Stonefish

Sara Antill

WINDMILL
BOOKS

New York

Published in 2011 by Windmill Books, LLC
303 Park Avenue South, Suite # 1280, New York, NY 10010-3657

First Edition

CREDITS:
Author: Sara Antill
Edited by: Jennifer Way
Designed by: Brian Garvey

Photo Credits: Cover © ARCO/H Frei/age fotostock; pp. 4–5, 5 (top), 6, 7, 8, 10, 12, 17, 19, 22 (top) Shutterstock.com; p. 5 (bottom) © www.iStockphoto.com/Achim Prill; pp. 9 (top), 13 (bottom) © www.iStockphoto.com/Dan Schmitt; p. 9 (bottom) © Alberto Carrera/age fotostock; p. 11 © www.iStockphoto.com/Steven Hayes; pp. 13 (top), 14, 22 (bottom) David Doubilet/National Geographic/Getty Images; p. 15 (top) © www.iStockphoto.com/Wieslaw Masztalerz; p. 15 (bottom) © www.iStockphoto.com/Oliver Hamalainen; pp. 16, 18 Jeff Rotman/Getty Images; p. 20 © www.iStockphoto.com/Paul Erickson; p. 21 © SuperStock, Inc.

Library of Congress Cataloging-in-Publication Data

Antill, Sara.
 Stonefish / by Sara Antill. — 1st ed.
    p. cm. — (Unusual animals)
 Includes index.
 ISBN 978-1-60754-992-5 (library binding) — ISBN 978-1-60754-999-4 (pbk.) — ISBN 978-1-61533-000-3 (6-pack)
 1. Stonefishes—Juvenile literature. I. Title.
 QL638.S42A68 2011
 597'.68—dc22
                              2010004432

Manufactured in the United States of America

For more great fiction and nonfiction, go to windmillbooks.com.

CPSIA Compliance Information: Batch # BW2011WM: For Further Information contact Windmill Books, New York, New York at 1-866-478-0556

Table of Contents

Fish or Rock?

The stonefish is a very strange-looking fish. It is very dangerous, too. The **poisonous** spines on its back make it the deadliest fish in the world.

Stonefish live in the warm waters of the Pacific Ocean and the Indian Ocean. They are usually dark brown or green. They may have orange, red, or yellow patches, too.

If you think this looks like a rock, look again! It's a stonefish sitting on the ocean floor.

Stonefish hide so well that you might have trouble seeing one, even if it is right in front of you. On the ocean floor, the stonefish looks just like another rock, or stone. In fact, that's how it got its name!

Australia's famous Great Barrier Reef is one place stonefish can be found.

People often mistake a stonefish for a rock. If they step on the fish, they are in for a surprise, and a nasty sting!

The stonefish uses **camouflage** to hide. Camouflage is a way of hiding in which an animal looks like the things around it. Stonefish look a lot like the rocks and **coral** pieces they live among.

7

The algae on a stonefish's skin doesn't hurt it. The algae helps the fish blend in with the rocks around it.

A stonefish doesn't have **scales** like many other fish. Its smooth skin is covered with crusty bumps that look like warts. The skin also can be covered with a layer of slime or **algae**.

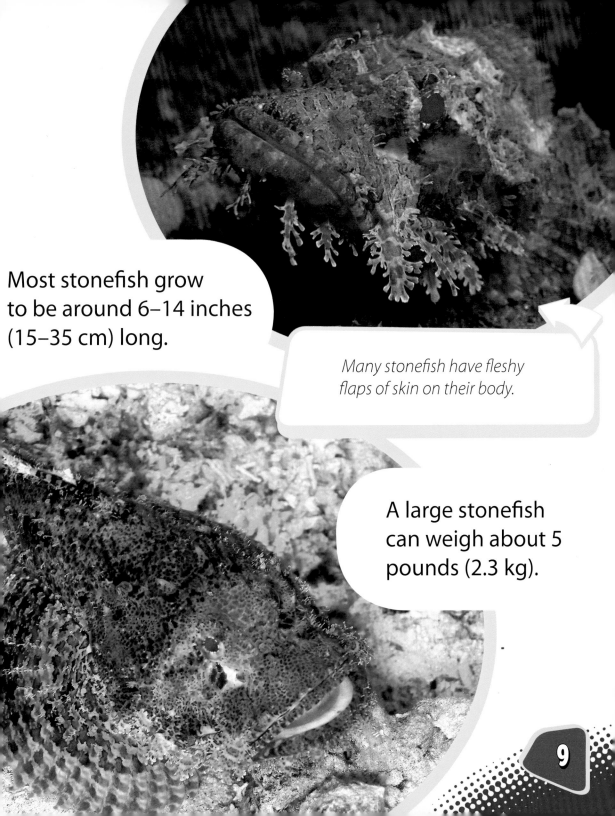

Most stonefish grow to be around 6–14 inches (15–35 cm) long.

Many stonefish have fleshy flaps of skin on their body.

A large stonefish can weigh about 5 pounds (2.3 kg).

Stonefish live mostly in shallow water. When the **tide** goes out, they can become trapped in small pools, called tide pools.

This is a tide pool in Tasmania, an island near Australia.

Sometimes, the **reefs** where stonefish live can dry up completely before the tide comes back again. Luckily for the stonefish, it can live without water for more than six hours!

Deadly Spines

Stonefish have 13 sharp spines on their back. These spines release poisonous **venom** when they are touched.

If you are in the water where stonefish live, be careful! Wear water shoes and watch where you step.

This usually happens when a person is walking in the water.

This is one of the stonefish's 13 sharp spines.

They might think they are stepping on a rock, but they are really stepping on a deadly stonefish!

Venomous spines

The stonefish doesn't swim away when it senses danger nearby. Instead, it makes sure its venomous spines are standing up.

A stonefish's venom causes swelling and lots of pain. The venom is so strong that many people who have been stung have died before they could get help from doctors.

Stonefish use their poisonous spines for **self-defense**.

Stonefish spend their time in water that isn't too deep

Larger animals can take one look at a stonefish's spines and know that they should stay away.

A Patient Hunter

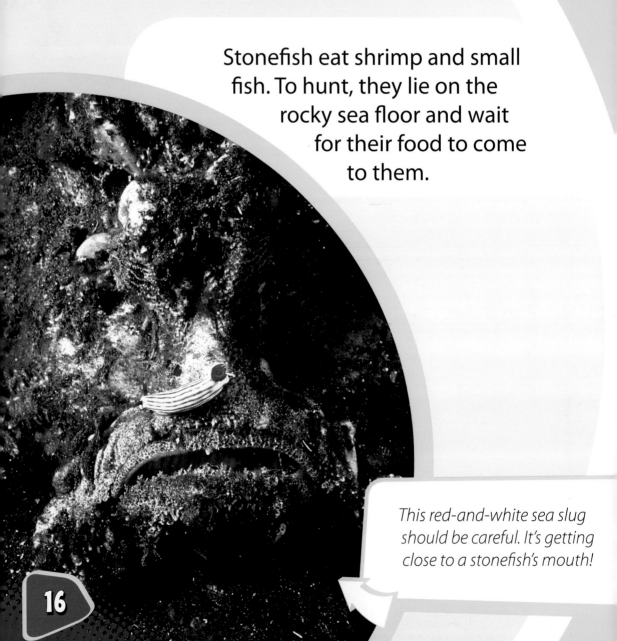

Stonefish eat shrimp and small fish. To hunt, they lie on the rocky sea floor and wait for their food to come to them.

This red-and-white sea slug should be careful. It's getting close to a stonefish's mouth!

When a smaller fish gets too close, the stonefish will grab the **prey** in its mouth and swallow it whole. This happens in less than a second. It is so fast that people need special high-speed cameras to see it!

A stonefish's eyes are near the top of its head. This helps the stonefish see more of what is around it as it lies on the bottom of the ocean.

This red stonefish is sitting on the ocean floor. It's waiting for its next meal to swim by.

This stonefish has covered its body with sand.

Stonefish have a wide fin on each side of their body. They use these fins to dig into the ocean floor and bury themselves in the mud. This makes it even harder for other fish to see them.

Some animals, like sharks and rays, eat stonefish. Young, small stonefish are sometimes eaten by large sea snakes.

This stonefish is being kept in an aquarium.

Scuba divers need to be careful in the water. They may accidentally touch a stonefish's spines.

Some people keep stonefish in their **aquariums**. In some parts of the world, people even eat stonefish. But they have to be very careful not to touch the sharp, deadly spines!

Inside Story

The largest stonefish ever caught was 20 inches (51 cm) long.

Stonefish stay perfectly still, even when a larger animal comes near them. Their only response to danger is to raise their poisonous spines.

Native people in Australia perform a dance that is hundreds of years old. In the dance, a fisherman pretends to step on a stonefish and die.

Glossary

ALGAE (AL-gee) Plants that live in the water and have no roots, stems, or leaves.

AQUARIUM (uh-KWAIR-ee-um) A man-made tank or pond that is filled with water in which fish and other marine animals are kept.

CAMOUFLAGE (KAM-uh-flaj) To hide by blending in with the surroundings.

CORAL (KOR-ul) Skeletal material from marine organisms that gathers on the ocean floor and looks like brightly colored rocks.

POISON (POY-zin) A substance that can hurt or kill a living being.

PREY (PRAY) An animal that is hunted and eaten by another animal.

REEF (REEF) An area near the surface of water that is covered with rocks and coral.

SCALES (SKAYLZ) Small, thin plates that cover the skin of many types of fish and reptiles.

SELF-DEFENSE (SELF-dee-FENS) Protecting yourself from an attack.

TIDE (TYD) The movement of ocean water caused by gravity from the Moon or Sun pulling on the Earth.

VENOM (VEH-num) A poison that some animals can release by biting or stinging.

Index

Read More

Clarke, Ginjer L. *Freak Out!: Animals Beyond Your Wildest Imagination*. New York: Grosset & Dunlap, 2006.

Earle, Sylvia. *Coral Reefs*. Des Moines, IA: National Geographic Children's Books, 2009.

Goldish, Meish. *Stonefish: Needles of Pain*. New York: Bearport Publishing, 2009.

Web Sites

For Web resources related to the subject of this book, go to: www.windmillbooks.com/weblinks and select this book's title.

24